THE MYSTERY OF NAN MADOL

PETER LACEY

Alphabet Publishing

www.AlphabetPublish.com

The huge, ancient city of Nan Madol was built of massive slabs of stone 1,000 years ago on the small island of Pohnpei, Micronesia. The facts of its origin are limited, and the construction method is mysterious; there is no written history nor good evidence to prove how it was built or who lived there. Today, this abandoned city is both an amazing example of what ancient humans could do with few resources and a megalithic mystery ripe for speculation.

How exactly was it built?

INTRODUCTION

The mysterious Nan Madol is in the middle of the Pacific Ocean. It's on an island called Pohnpei, part of a group of other small islands called Micronesia. This is a place thousands of miles away from Asia and the Americas. Few places are more isolated, and this isolation means understanding the full history of the islands and their cultures is difficult.

Nan Madol itself is a very old city made entirely of huge pieces of stone. Most of them are quite long with flat sides like slabs. There are so many huge pieces of stone that it's clear the construction was a complex operation. Although it is no longer inhabited, visitors can walk among and explore many of the impressive walls and structures that are still standing and consider the mystery of the stone construction up close.

Given the lack of historical record, we're left to guess how the city was completed in the days before advanced machinery. This is the main mystery: Who exactly did this and how did they overcome the challenges of building such an extensive stone city on the small, isolated island?

Introductory Questions

1. Have you ever heard of Micronesia or Nan Madol? What do you already know?

2. Have you ever visited the Pacific Ocean and any of its islands? Describe your experience OR tell about an island you hope to visit someday.

3. What are the oldest physical structures in your area? How old are they and who built them?

CONTENTS

THE PLACE

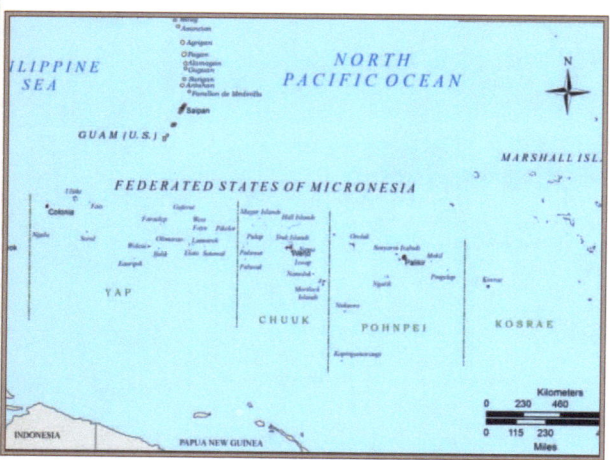

The vast Pacific Ocean covers nearly a third of earth's surface. What may look like a huge area of empty, uninhabited territory on a map actually contains many of our planet's most incredible features. It is a place where you will find volcanoes creating brand new, tar-black coastlines from lava. It is home to the Marianas Trench, the deepest spot on earth at nearly 7 miles below the surface of the ocean. It is also the location where birds called bar-tailed godwits make 11,000 mile migrations between New Zealand and Alaska. On the northern edges you can find brown bears fishing for salmon, and in the south you can find penguins bringing food up from beneath the ocean's waves to their nests on land. All across the Pacific Ocean, there are amazing things to witness.

The Pacific Ocean is also dotted with many islands. We know some of these islands as picturesque vacation spots, surfing meccas, or the sites of historical battles. Some places, such as the Hawaiian Islands, qualify for all of those categories! But one island in particular has a unique mystery that makes it special among

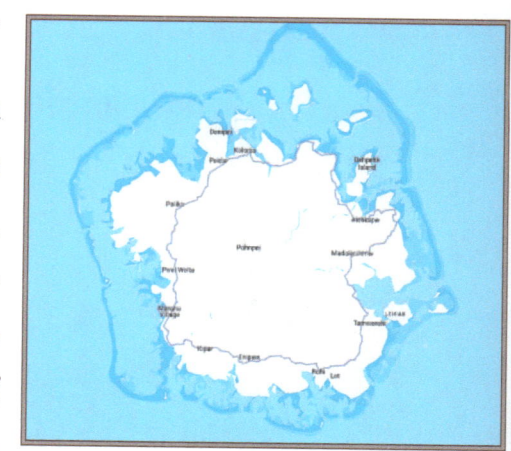

all the other Pacific islands. This special island is Pohnpei, the home to an ancient stone city called Nan Madol.

Pohnpei is one of four island states in the Federated States of Micronesia (FSM), which is a very small nation about halfway between Hawaii and the Philippines. If you look for Pohnpei on a map or globe, all you will find is a very small dot near the middle of the Pacific, far from any of the larger islands. But that dot is home to the capital city, Palikir, and many spectacular natural features.

Pohnpei is a tropical island and visitors can expect hot, humid weather and sudden rain storms while they explore the steep, jungle-covered mountains and rain-fed rivers that crash over dark rocks. Even though it is an island, there are not many sandy beaches on its coast. In most places, the trees and rocks go right down to the water. But visitors will be able to enjoy other spectacular features like

MICRONESIA

Micronesia is the name for four different groups of islands between Hawaii and the Philippines. These islands are controlled by several different countries. The Marianas Islands in the north contain the U.S.-controlled Guam. The Gilbert Islands in the southeast are where you find the nation of Kiribati (pronounced Kir-ih-BASS). In the northeast, the Marshall Islands make up another independent nation. And in the center of Micronesia are the Caroline Islands, which contain both the island nation Palau and The Federated States of Micronesia.

The Federated States of Micronesia contain many islands, but the nation is divided into four main island states: Chuuk, Kosrae, Pohnpei, and Yap. Although Pohnpei is the home of Nan Madol and the capital city Palikir, the other islands are also important for understanding the history and culture of Micronesian people. For example, the history of Yap includes the unique use of carved stone money called Rai Stones. Chuuk has the biggest population and is the site of an underwater cemetery of sunken Japanese ships from World War II. And Kosrae, the smallest state, also contains an ancient stone city called Leluh.

Historians think the first people who lived in FSM arrived from other islands several thousand years ago. These first people developed their own societies including beliefs, customs, leaders, and towns on the islands. And eventually, the Saudeleur Dynasty on Pohnpei led to a society so advanced it could construct Nan Madol.

European explorers didn't arrive in the islands until hundreds of years after the construction of Nan Madol. Spain was the first European empire to control the islands in the 19th century, but they gave control to Germany in 1899. After World War I, Japan took control, but they had to give control to the United States after losing World War II. The current nation of FSM claimed independence from the United States in 1979.

Sokehs Rock, Kepirohi Waterfall, and, of course, the ancient city Nan Madol.

THE CITY

The ruins of Nan Madol are one of the most famous sites on Pohnpei. You can find this ancient city on the eastern coast of the island. Nobody has lived there for hundreds of years, and it is partially overgrown by palm trees, breadfruit trees, and other plants climbing over the site. But visitors today can walk around some of the buildings and walls and marvel at the impressive construction. When you approach the ruins, the smooth, angular geometry of man-made structures becomes clear. Walls of black basalt rise out of the mangroves. The long pieces of stone are stacked high, with each layer crossing the previous at 90 degrees. Looking closely, it is obvious the stone columns were cut to fit together. The largest of these walls tower far above

your head, and you can climb to the top of some to survey the city. From the top of the walls, you can see how the ocean water flows in and surrounds many of the buildings during high tide. The structures serve as small artificial islands, and the walls create long, straight canals. There are 98 island structures at the site, and though it is called a city, the design of the larger walls and canals resembles something like a fortress. When you see the site in person, it is clear the extensive city was carefully designed with a lot of planning and hard work.

THE HISTORY

Historians think Nan Madol was built during the Saudeleur Dynasty close to 1,000 years ago (around 1200 AD). They have found that some of

the larger buildings were built to be the tombs of rulers, and they have found more evidence that important political ceremonies also happened in the city. The site was probably not big enough for all the people on the island to live in but was mostly a special place for the activities of the Saudeleur Dynasty's priests and rulers.

Because there is no recorded history from this time, it is difficult to know exactly which people lived there and what everyday life looked like inside the basalt walls. Historians aren't sure about those details. Furthermore, just like Stonehenge or the pyramids of Egypt, nobody knows exactly how the ancient people managed to construct something so impressive. There are no blueprints or plans from that time, and everything we know comes either from examination by archaeologists or the legendary stories that have been told by people living on the island.

People who make plans for large construction projects are called engineers, and the engineers for the Saudeleur Dynasty had to be very smart. They designed and constructed Nan Madol with limited resources. You can imagine all the tools and big machines you would see at a construction site today—cranes to lift heavy pieces, machines to dig and trucks to haul dirt, and jackhammers and welding torches—but the people who built Nan Madol did not have the help of any of that modern technology. What tools would they have been able to use 1,000 years ago?

The project seems even more difficult when you realize it was done by a small civilization that was practically isolated in the middle of a huge ocean. They didn't have all the land, natural resources, or manpower that civilizations on the continents used

Colossal head from the Olmec civilization

Easter Island *mohai* statue

WHAT ARE MEGALITHS?

Megaliths are ancient monuments or structures that were built with very large stones. These monuments can be found in many countries around the world. In fact, you might not be very far from the site of a megalith right now as you read.

Some megaliths are made from just one rock carved to look like a human, such as the *moai* statues on Easter Island or Olmec colossal heads in Mexico. Others are simple structures called dolmens that mark grave sites in Europe and Asia. One well-known megalith is Stonehenge in England, which averages 800,000 visitors per year. But every megalithic site, no matter how famous, is an interesting glimpse into the ancient world. People like to marvel at these sites and wonder about the life and rituals of the ancient cultures that constructed the megaliths.

Historians and archaeologists study these sites to understand our ancient cultures, but megaliths keep many mysteries. It's not always clear why or how they were built. Different sites may have been used for astronomy, religion, or communication, but the people who built them rarely left any information about how they built them or any description of

Simple *dolmen*, South Korea

11

what they did there. We often have to guess using limited evidence. Archaeologists continue to make new discoveries that build our knowledge of these places and help us understand the people who made them.

Part of the intrigue of megaliths is the idea that such very large stones could have been carved, transported, and lifted into the air without any modern machinery. Because we don't know exactly how it was done at some sites, people sometimes wonder if these ancient cultures used advanced technology that we don't have anymore. However it was done, it seems clear that megalithic sites were very important because of all the time and energy that was necessary to build them.

to construct their incredible ancient sites. It is a very impressive feat for an island civilization and suggests there are many things we don't know about the Saudeleur Dynasty and their power and capabilities.

Some of the stories about Nan Madol say the builders came from another island or civilization. But if the knowledge and skill to build Nan Madol didn't come from the people of Pohnpei, then it is difficult to know exactly where it did come from. The other islands near Pohnpei in Micronesia are also very small and remote, so it doesn't seem likely they would have access to better technology or information. Larger civilizations in Asia and the Americas had a lot of experience building impressive stone cities and structures, but they would have had to have made an incredibly long and difficult journey across the ocean, and there is no evidence this happened.

If Nan Madol's engineers arrived on Pohnpei after a voyage across the ocean, we don't know where they came from or how the voyage was made. As far as we can tell, Nan Madol was planned and built by a relatively small group of people from remote Pacific islands.

Perhaps the biggest mystery of Nan Madol's construction is how the people overcame the physical challenge of cutting and moving the massive pieces of stone. There is no quarry or other source for the stone near Nan Madol, which means all of the stones were moved long distance from somewhere else—probably the other side of the island. We know that the stone is basalt, a dark volcanic rock, and there is a lot of basalt across the island from Nan Madol. Of course, the stones also had to be cut to the right length and carved to fit together correctly. How could the ancient islanders have cut the rock so precisely and moved piece after

piece across the jungle mountains and into place at the city site without the help of modern machines? It would have required not just very smart engineers but also very skilled and strong workers.

The city is such an incredible achievement that some people have said its construction was done by magic. There are legends that magicians moved the big rocks across the island by making them float through the air. It would have been an unbelievably fantastic scene to see columns of stone flying across the green jungle like a flock of giant birds or squadron of airplanes. Of course, historians and archaeologists are very skeptical of those stories of magic, and most of us today would guess the Saudeleur Dynasty did not use magic, but instead had a very good understanding of the laws of physics. Nevertheless, these stories highlight what a fantastic achievement the city was and how awe-inspiring it is to the people who have seen it.

You can travel the many miles across the ocean to Pohnpei by airplane today. And you can put your hand on the walls of Nan Madol and feel how sturdy and heavy the pieces are. When you do, it's easy to realize that people everywhere on earth have been doing amazing, smart things with great skill for a very long time—not just in China, England, or Egypt, but on tiny islands in the middle of the Pacific Ocean. Like historians and archaeologists, you may want to know how—how it was done way back then, way out in the ocean.

Only the ancient people of Pohnpei know the answers for sure, but historians, archaeologists, and visitors to Pohnpei remain curious about the facts of the amazing megalithic city, Nan Madol.

Temwen Island

Peinkitel

Kohnderek

Usen dahu

Dau

Nan Dowas

Pah

Pahn Kadira

Dapahu

Peinering

Powe

reef

Kariahn

Idedh

Darong

Kelepwei

Pahnwi

Nan Madol

m 100 200

LEARN MORE

"Nan Madol: The City Built on Coral Reefs", Christopher Pala:
https://www.smithsonianmag.com/history/an-madol-the-city-built-on-coral-reefs-147288758

"Nan Madol", Jennifer Wagelie: https://www.metmuseum.org/toah/hd/nmad/hd_nmad.htm

Nan-Madol, Pohnepi Visitor's Bureau: https://www.nan-madol.com

THE THEORIES

Special Technology: Some people who learn about Nan Madol and marvel at its mystery suggest the engineers of the Saudeleur dynasty must have used special tools or techniques that we no longer understand. They think that because the construction is a mystery to us today, the people who did it must have known things we no longer know. Those things could have been special tools or advanced understanding of physics.

This theory is not unique to Nan Madol but often speculated for many mega-lithic sites we don't fully understand. It is not a theory strongly supported by science or historians because there is not good evidence for special, advanced technology in the Saudeleur Dynasty.

Visitors: The story of the magician brothers claims they came from a foreign land. Even though some people don't believe they used magic, they think it is likely the builders of Nan Madol did come from another culture and brought their construction skills with them. The Leluh site on Kosrae is claimed as evidence that construction technology was being shared across the ocean.

Although archaeologists believe Nan Madol was built before Leluh, they agree it is likely these two sites on different islands were built with technology from the same culture. There are many different places this technology could have come from, but there is no good evidence that shows a connection to a culture outside Micronesia.

Supernatural Power: Some people from Pohnpei tell a story of two brothers who were magicians. They used their magic powers to build Nan Madol. Their most fantastic act was making the rocks fly through the air from one side of the island to the other.

People who support this theory believe the construction was not possible without supernatural power and believe the laws of physics and archaeology cannot explain everything about Nan Madol's construction. Because there is no good evidence of the tools and technology used, they believe it was something else—magic! However, people who trust science will argue there is also no good evidence of magic at Nan Madol (or anywhere else in history).

WHY DOES IT MATTER?

Nan Madol is a site of immense historical, cultural, and scientific importance, offering valuable insights into ancient Micronesian civilization and contributing to our understanding of human ingenuity and adaptability.

FUN FACTS

It's All In the Name: The name Nan Madol translates to "In the space between things," which is a reference to the canals that surround the stone structures.

UNESCO World Heritage Site: In 2016, Nan Madol was designated a UNESCO World Heritage Site. It was also added to the list of World Heritage in Danger due to its vulnerability to natural disasters and environmental degradation.

Pohnpeian Mythology: Local myths say that the city was built by twin sorcerers, Olisihpa and Olosohpa, who used magic to move the giant stones. These legends add an element of mystery and intrigue to the site's history.

Hollywood Inspiration: Nan Madol has inspired various fictional works and has been featured in several documentaries and TV shows, capturing the imagination of people fascinated by ancient mysteries and lost civilizations.

No Fresh Water: One of the unique aspects of Nan Madol is that there is no fresh water on the islets. Water had to be brought from the main island of Pohnpei, adding to the logistical challenges of living there.

Another Mysterious City: Nan Madol is not the only ancient stone city in Micronesia. In the state of Kosrae, a few hundred miles east of Pohnpei, you can visit the remains of a city that is very similar to Nan Madol. The city is on a small island called Lelu, and it is called the Leluh archeological site. Historians believe this city was built after Nan Madol, but the features are so similar that it seems likely the same people or same techniques and tools built both places.

Like Nan Madol, Leluh is constructed of large pieces of dark basalt stone, and it was probably built for priests and rulers. Even though scientists believe Leluh is not quite as old as Nan Madol, it is old enough that there is no recorded history of its construction. It, too, is an ancient megalithic mystery.

Images of the Leluh site in Micronesia

GLOSSARY

archaeologist (n.) — a person who studies ancient places to understand history

astronomy (n.) — the scientific study of stars and space

canal (n.) — a man-made passage for water

colossal (adj.) — large and incredible, especially statues

dynasty (n.) — a family of rulers

engineer (n.) — a person who plans and organizes construction

intrigue (n.) — interest because of unknown information

isolated (adj.) — alone and not close to others

magician (n.) — a person with supernatural ability

marvel (v.) — to think about with surprise or amazement

megalith (n.) — an ancient structure of large stones

monument (n.) — a structure built to remember or celebrate

precisely (adv.) — exactly, accurately in small details

priest (n.) — a person who is a religious leader

quarry (n.) — a place where rock is cut or taken from the earth

rituals (n.) — special traditions repeated regularly

skeptical (adj.) — to have doubt, unable to believe or trust

statues (n.) — a monument of a person or animal

tomb (n.) — a place underground for a dead body

DISCUSSION QUESTIONS

1. Which theory about Nan Madol is most likely?
   - Is magic a serious theory? Why would somebody believe in magic, and why do fewer people believe in magic now than in the past?

2. What do you think Nan Madol was like when people lived there?
   - What did the ancient people do there?

3. What compelled ancient civilizations to spend so much energy on megalithic construction?
   - Did these structures offer many practical benefits, or were they built for other reasons?

4. What physical structures in your area will remain for 1,000 years?
   - Will they still be in use?
   - Will people in the future be interested in the remains of our current architecture and social centers?
   - What will seem mysterious or odd to future people who study the remains of your city?

PROJECTS

1. Describe your own theory.
    - Write about one page to explain how you think Nan Madol was actually built.
    - Include details about who did it and what tools and methods were used for cutting stone and moving it long distance. How was all of this possible 1,000 years ago?

2. Design your own island city.
    - Draw a blueprint of your own special city. What buildings will you construct and what materials can you use? Imagine that you must use only the resources available on the island.

3. Research megaliths in your own country.
    - Choose one and find out what we know about who, where, when, why, and how it was built.
    - Create a poster or presentation to share your research.

4. Research a Pacific Island.
    - Look at a map of the Pacific ocean and choose an island to research.
    - What information can you find about the people, the history, and the natural features of the island?
    - Create a travel brochure to attract visitors who want to experience the island.

REFERENCES

Britannica. (1999, July 26). *Pacific Ocean*. Encyclopedia Britannica. https://www.britannica.com/place/Pacific-Ocean

History.com. (2010, June 1). *Stonehenge*. HISTORY. https://www.history.com/topics/british-history/stonehenge

Matairakula, L. (2023, April 17). *Discover Nan Madol: The ruined coral city*. Pacific Tourism Organisation. https://southpacificislands.travel/discover-nan-madol-the-ruined-coral-city/

McCaffery, B. J., & Gill, R. E. (2020, March 4). *Bar-tailed godwit (limosa lapponica), version 1.0. Birds of the World*. https://birdsoftheworld.org/bow/species/batgod/cur/introduction

McCoy, M. D., Alderson, H. A., Hemi, R., Cheng, H., & Edwards, R. L. (2016). Earliest direct evidence of monument building at the archaeological site of Nan Madol (Pohnpei, Micronesia) identified using 230th/u coral dating and geochemical sourcing of Megalithic Architectural Stone. Quaternary Research, 86(3), 295–303. https://doi.org/10.1016/j.yqres.2016.08.002

National Park Service. (2020, January 6). Nan Madol (U.S. National Park Service). NPS.gov (U.S. National Park Service). https://www.nps.gov/places/nan-madol.htm

Pala, C. (2009, November 3). *Nan Madol: The city built on coral reefs*. Smithsonian Magazine. https://www.smithsonianmag.com/history/nan-madol-the-city-built-on-coral-reefs-147288758/

Pohnpei Visitors Bureau. (n.d.). *About Nan Madol*. Nan Madol. https://www.nan-madol.com/

UNESCO World Heritage Centre. (n.d.). *Nan Madol: Ceremonial Centre of Eastern Micronesia*. UNESCO World Heritage Centre https://whc.unesco.org/en/list/1503/

Wagelie, J. (2002, October). *Nan Madol*. The Met's Heilbrunn Timeline of Art History. https://www.metmuseum.org/toah/hd/nmad/hd_nmad.htm

ISBN: 978-1-956159-56-1 (print)

For permission requests, write to the publisher at "ATTN: Permissions", at the address below:

29 Milo Dr. Branford, CT 06405 USA

info@alphabetpublishingbooks.com

www.AlphabetPublishingBooks.com

Discounts on class sets and bulk orders available upon inquiry.

Cover and Interior Design by Walton Burns

Country of Manufacture Specified on Last Page

First Printing 2025

Images

pg. ii top Wikimedia/CTSnow, CC-by-SA 2.0 • pg. ii bottom Wikimedia/Patrick Nunn, CC-by-SA 4.0 • pg. iv Wikimedia/Uhooep, CC-by-SA 4.0 • pg. 6 top Google Maps, Used by permission • pg. 6 bottom US Dept. of Agriculture, Public Domain • pg. 8 Wikimedia/Patrick Nunn, CC-by-SA 4.0 • pg. 9 top Wikimedia/CTSnow, CC-by-SA 2.0 • pg. 9 middle Wikimedia/CTSnow, CC-by-SA 2.0 • pg. 9 bottom Wikimedia/CTSnow, CC-by-SA 2.0 • pg. 11 top Wikimedia/Rick Champion, CC-by-SA 4.0 • pg. 11 middle Wikimedia/Mike W, CC-by-SA 2.0 • pg. 11 bottom Wikimedia/Taewangkorea, CC-by-SA 4.0 • pg. 12 DepositPhotos/StockShoppe, Used by permission • pg. 13 top Wikimedia/Patrick Nunn, CC-by-SA 4.0 • pg. 13 top middle Wikimedia/Uhooep, CC-by-SA 4.0 • pg. 13 bottom middle Wikimedia/Jebrennan, CC-by-SA 4.0 • pg. 13 bottom Wikimedia/CTSnow, CC-by-SA 2.0 • pg. 15 Wikimedia/Holbe, Public Domain • pg. 16 DepositPhotos/Vector 3D, Used by permission • pg. 19 right Wikimedia/Maloff1, CC-by-SA 3.0 • pg. 19 left Wikimedia/Maloff1, CC-by-SA 3.0

www.ingramcontent.com/pod-product-compliance
Lightning Source LLC
Chambersburg PA
CBHW041451120626
46547CB00002B/407